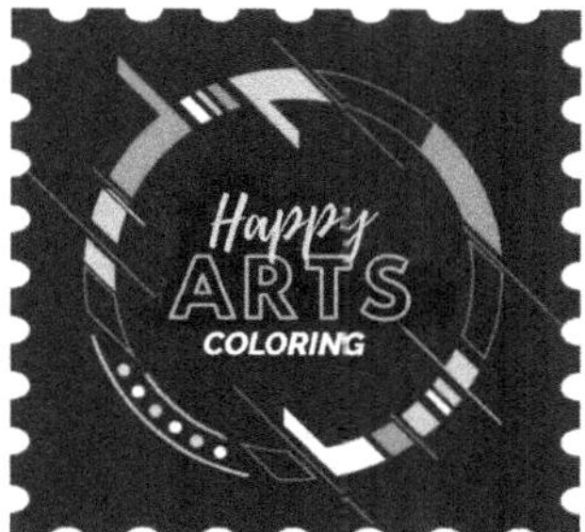

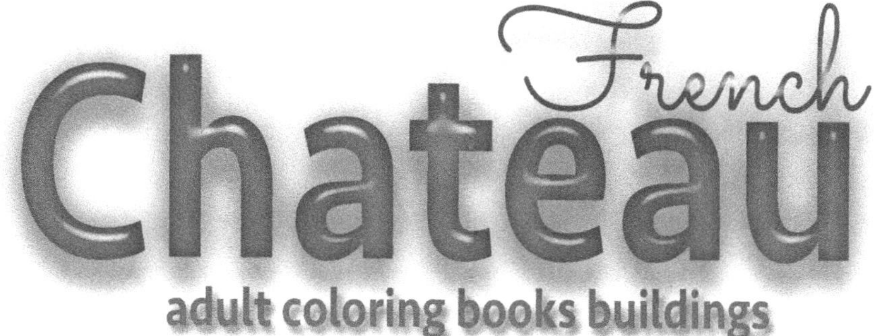

French Chateau

adult coloring books buildings

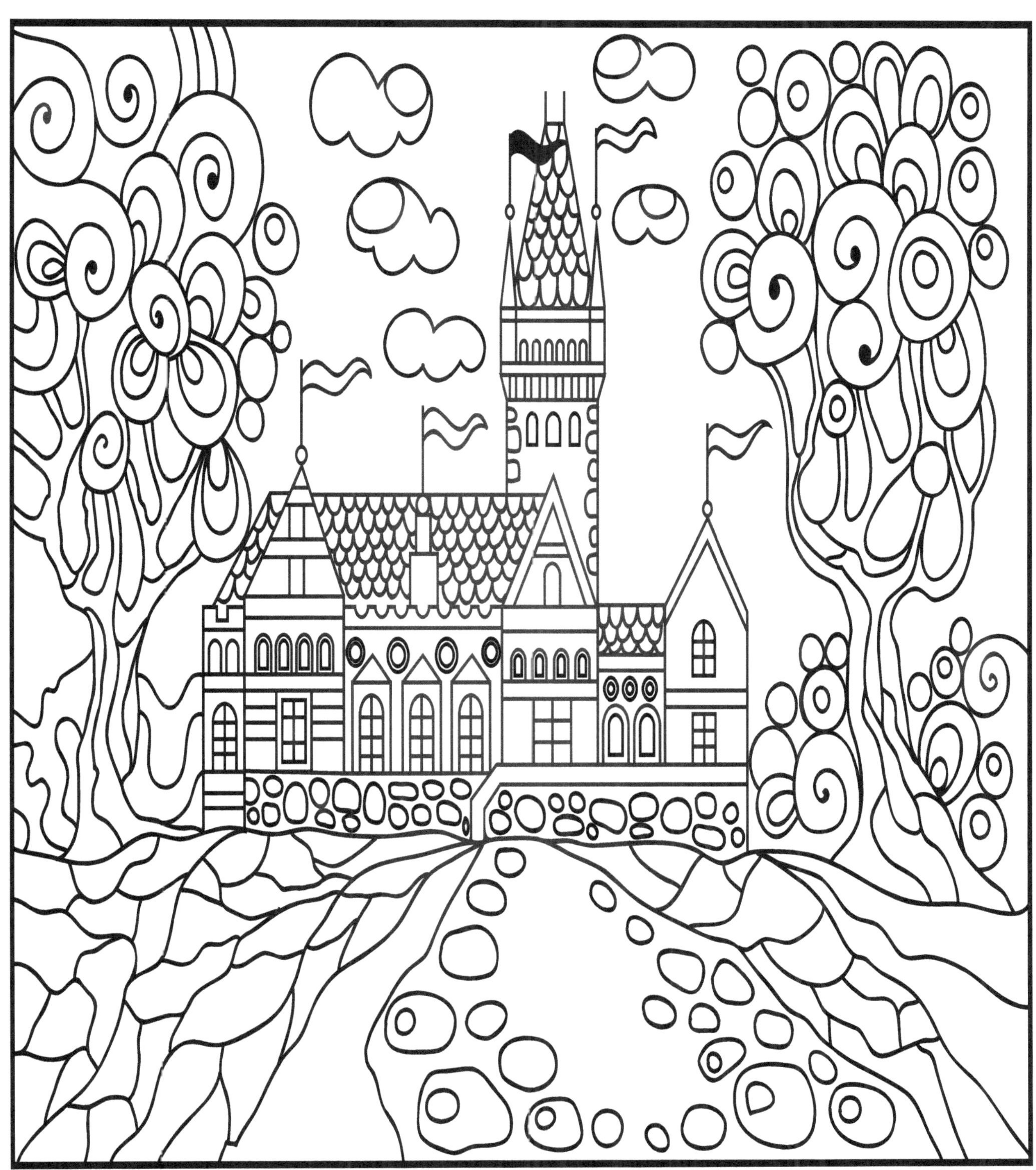

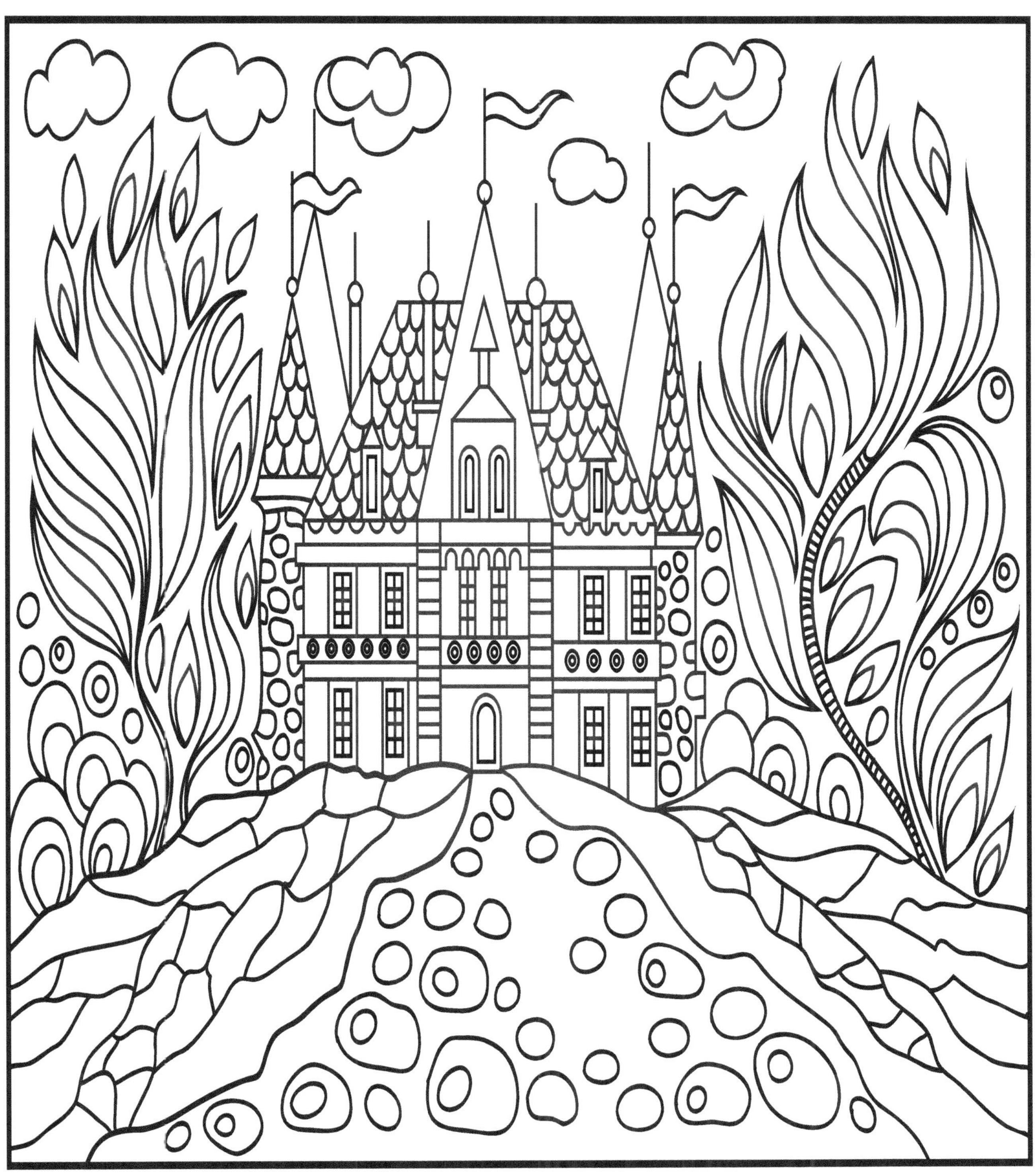

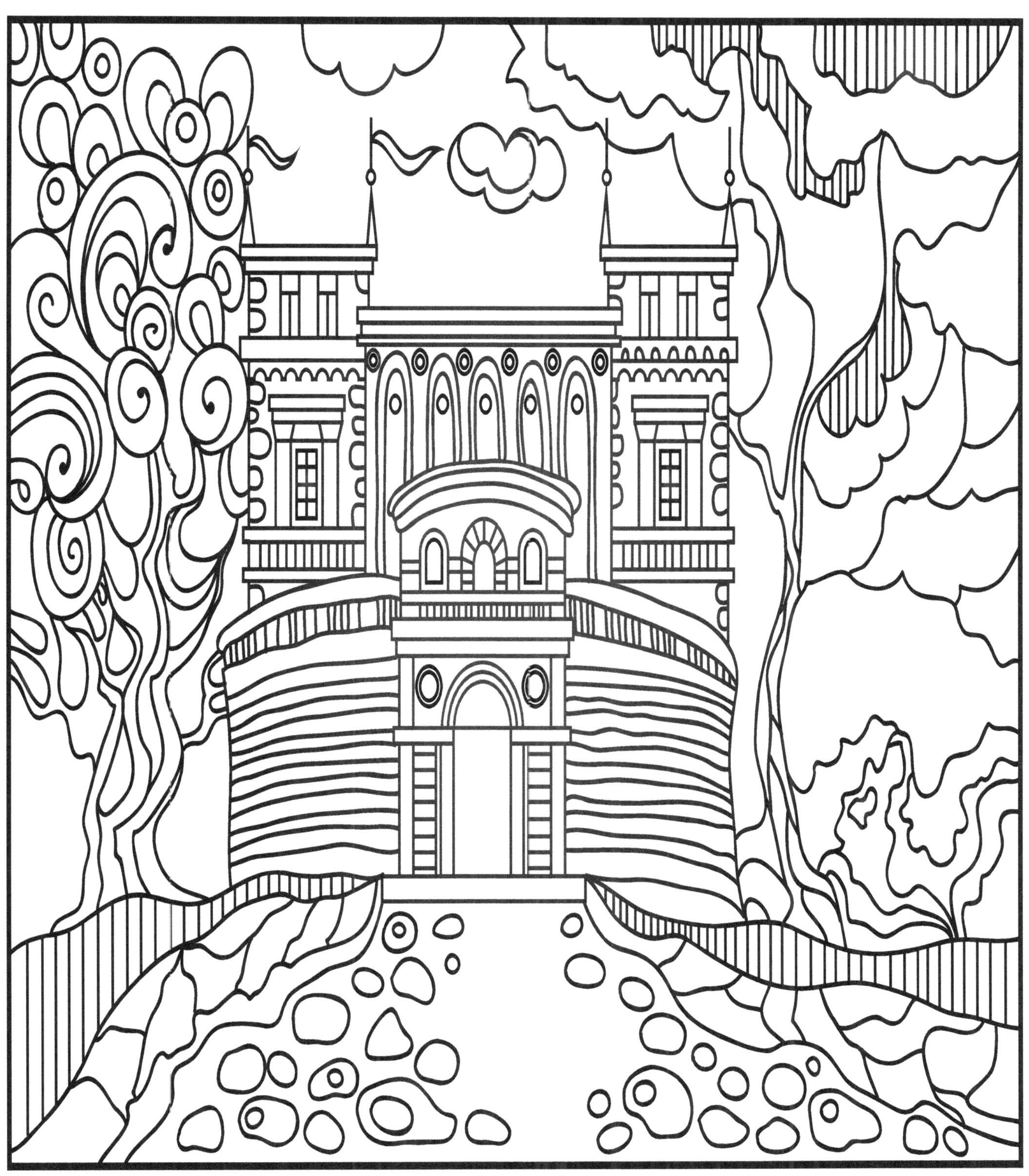

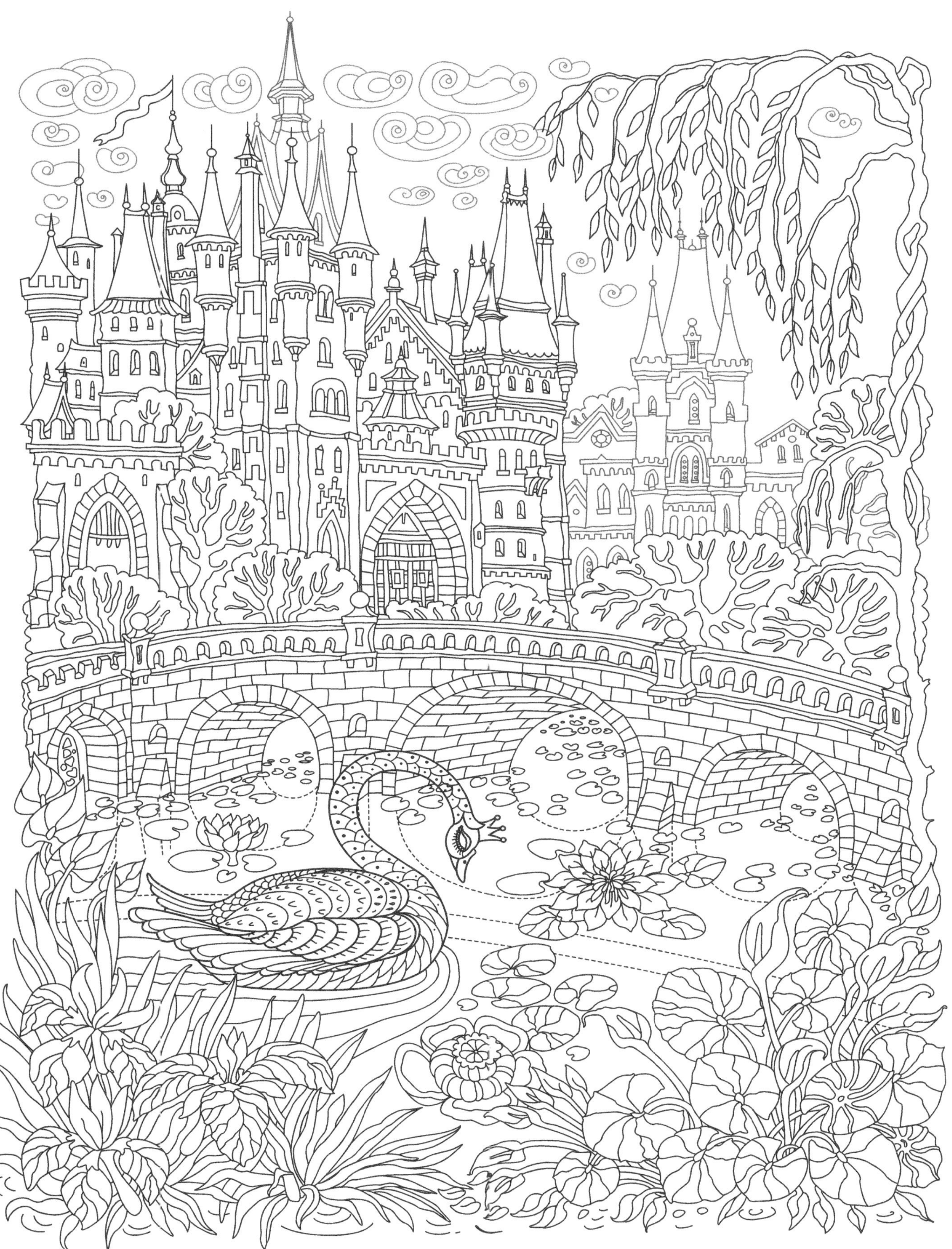

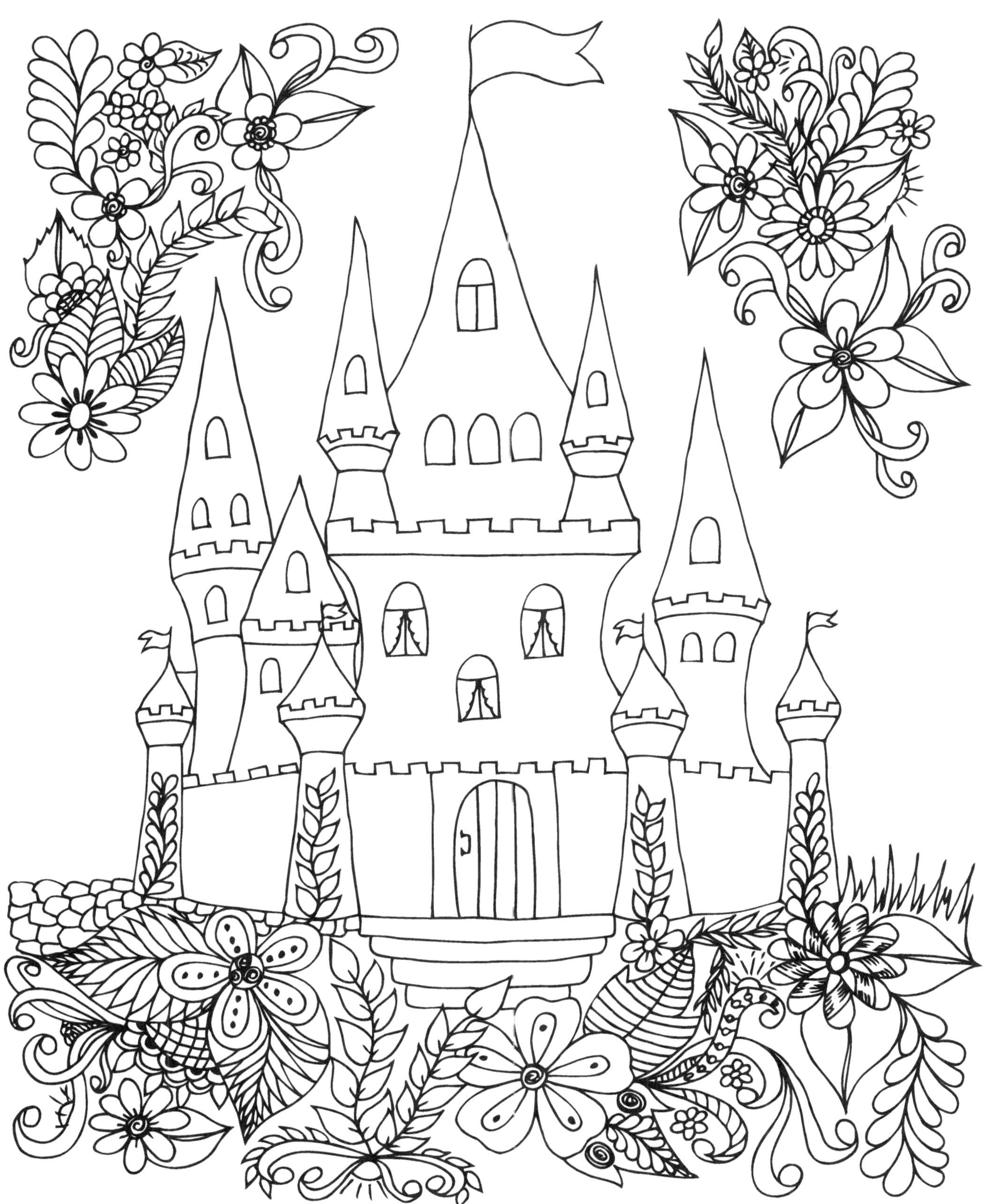

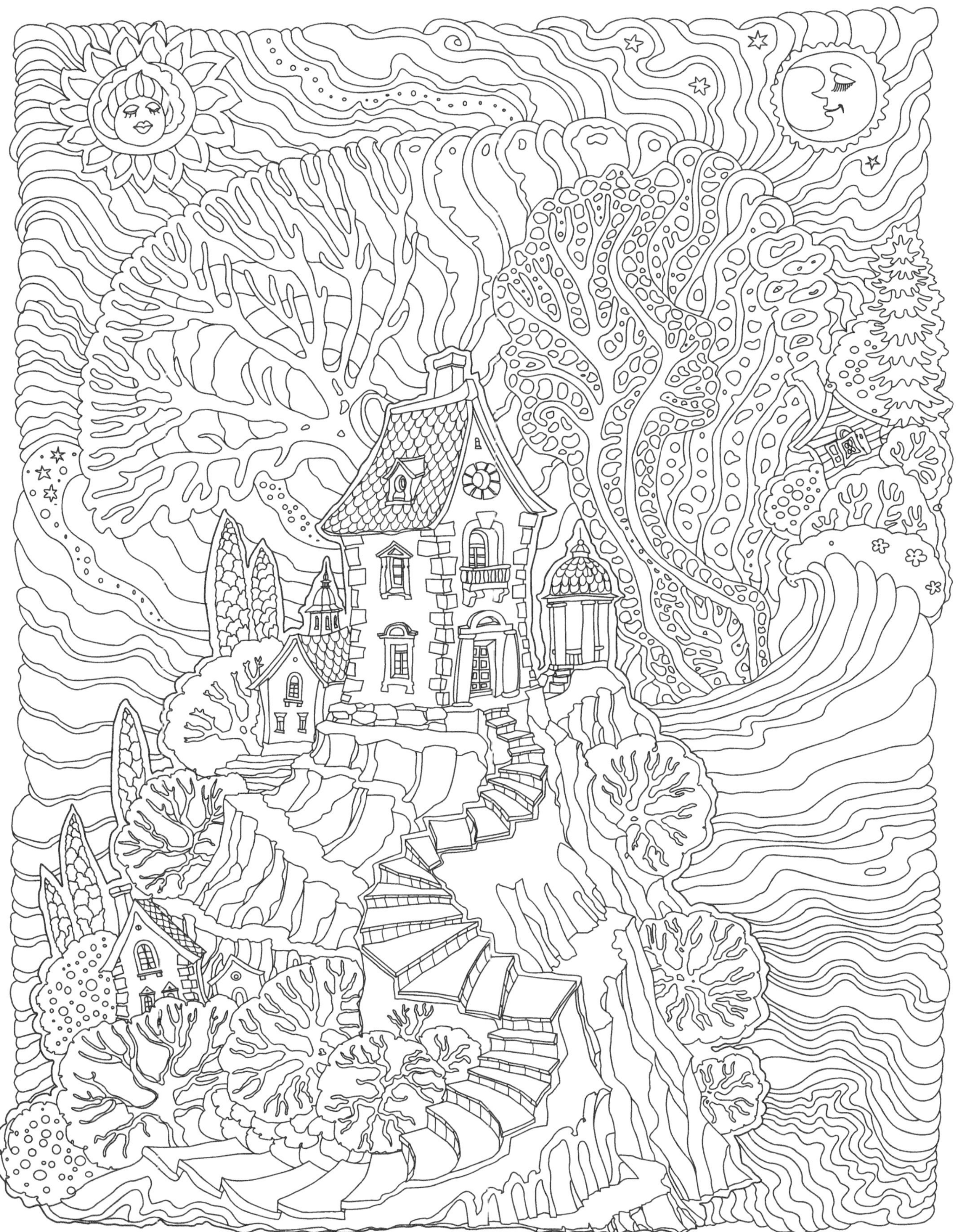

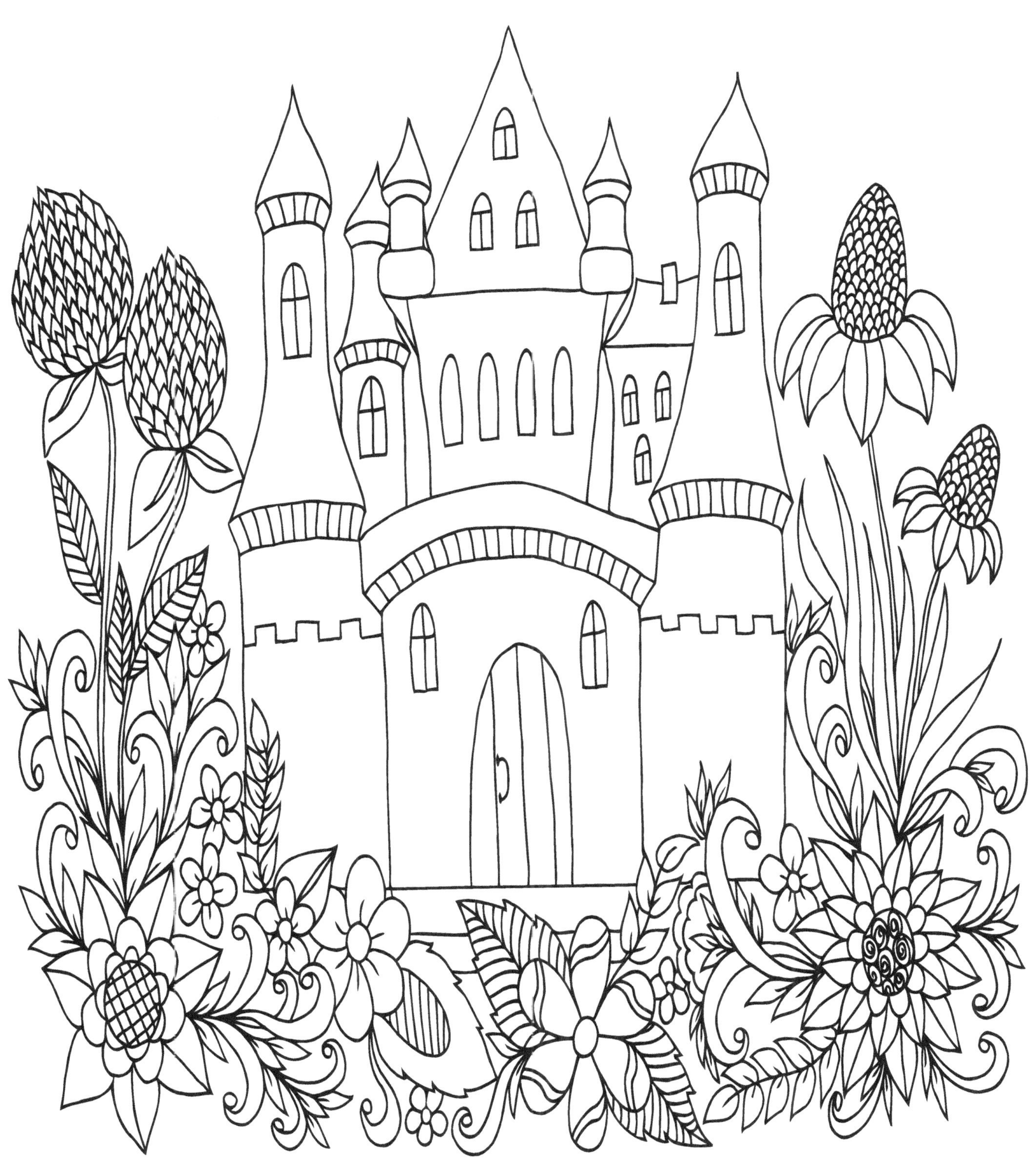

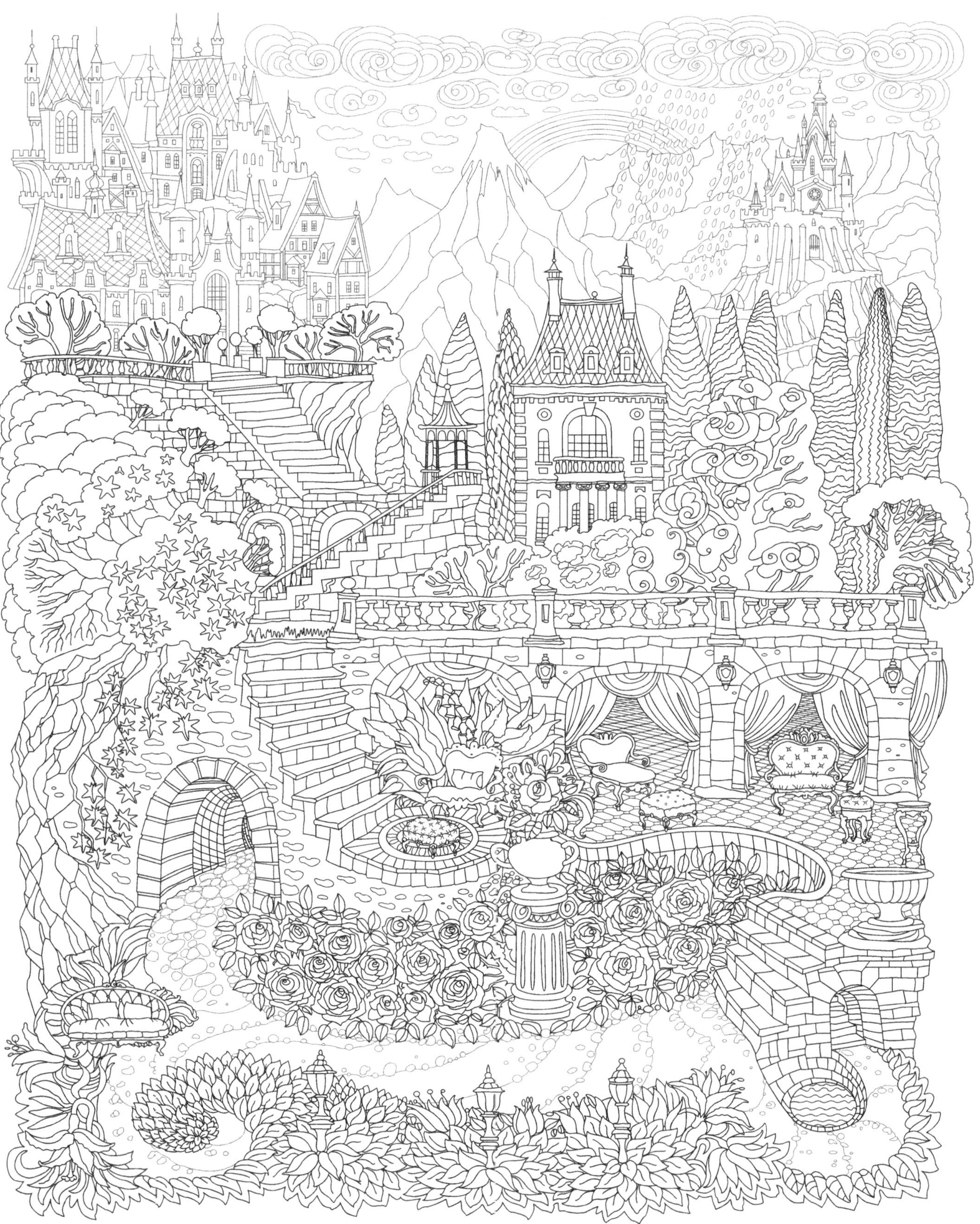

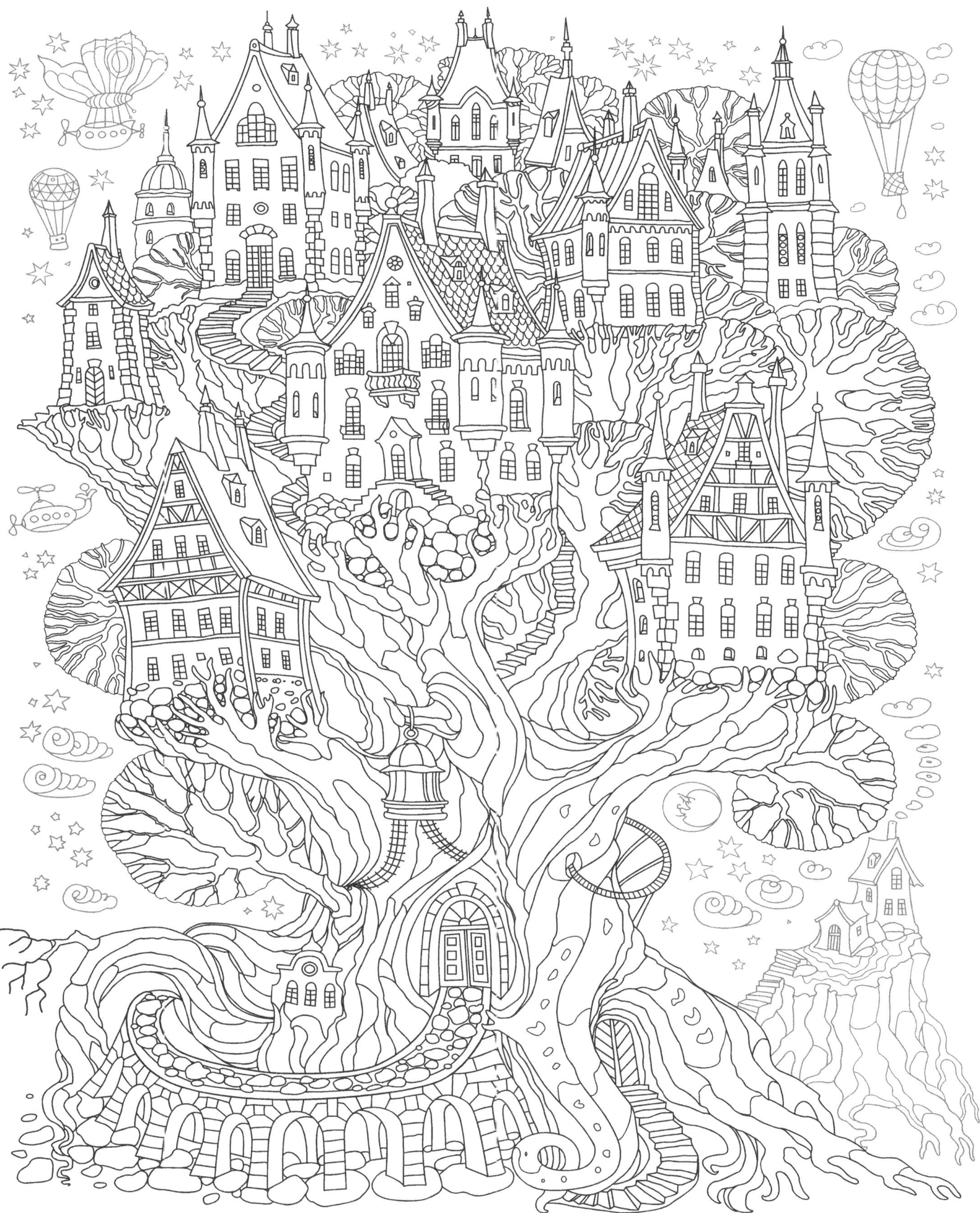

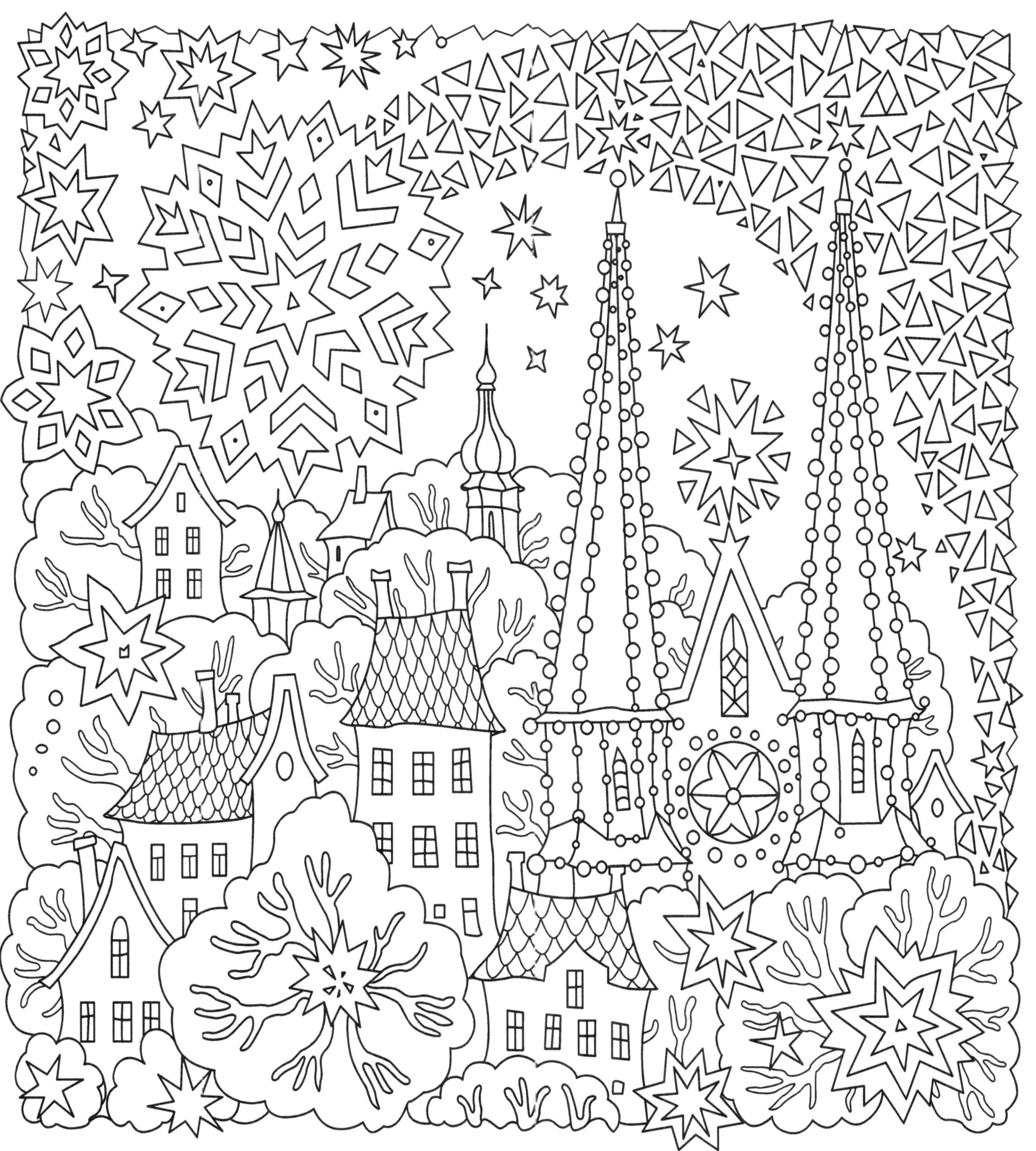

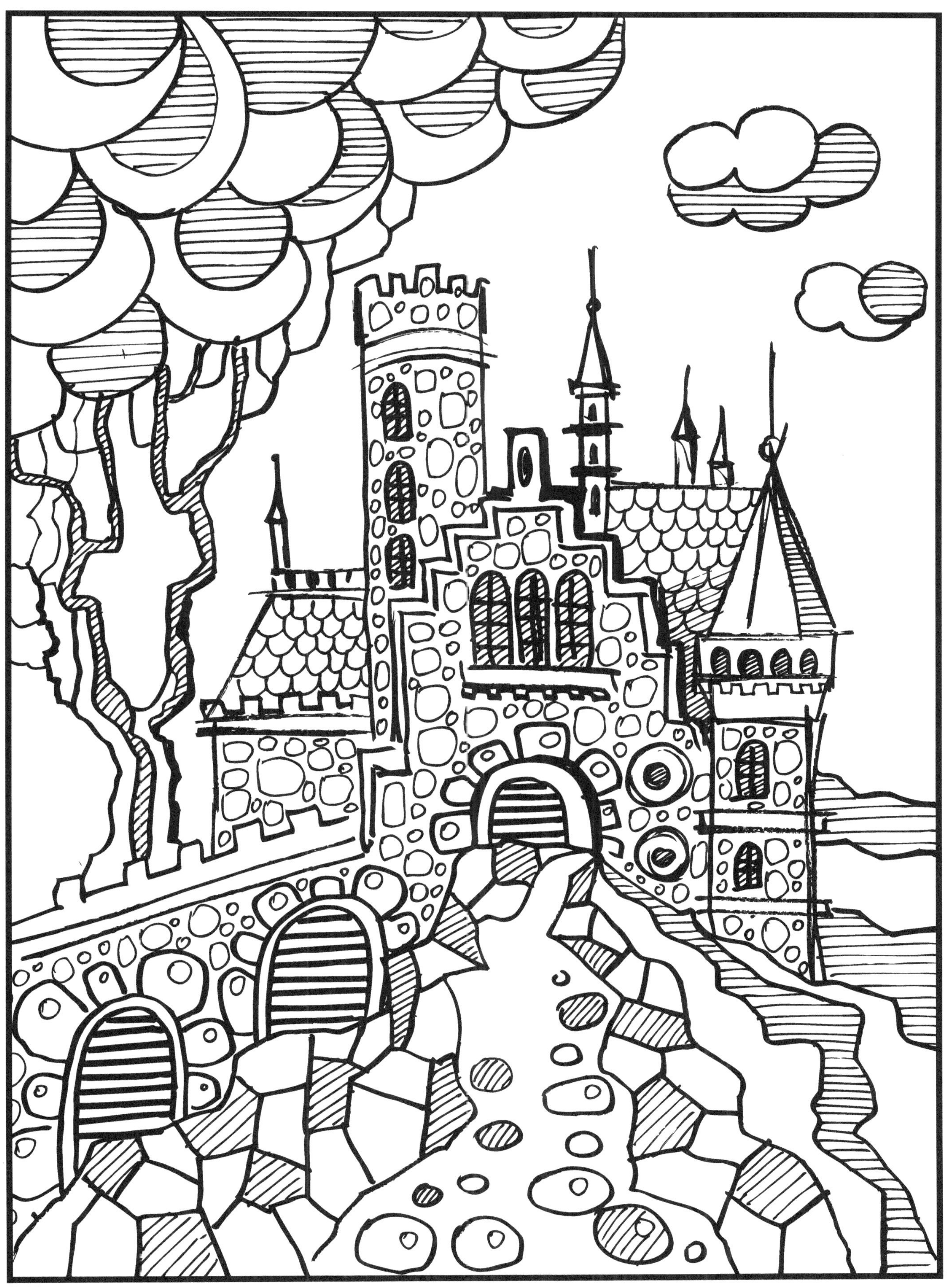

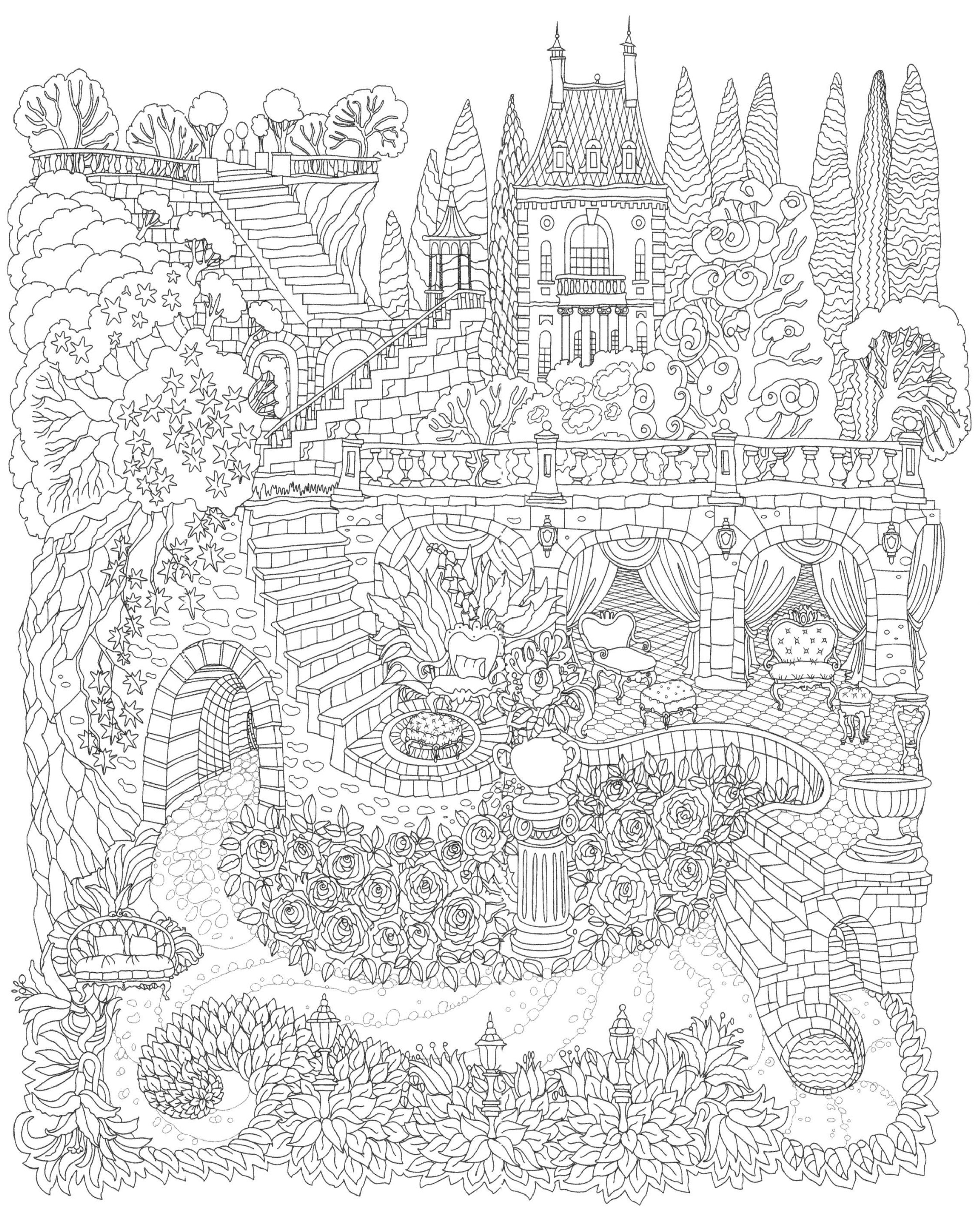

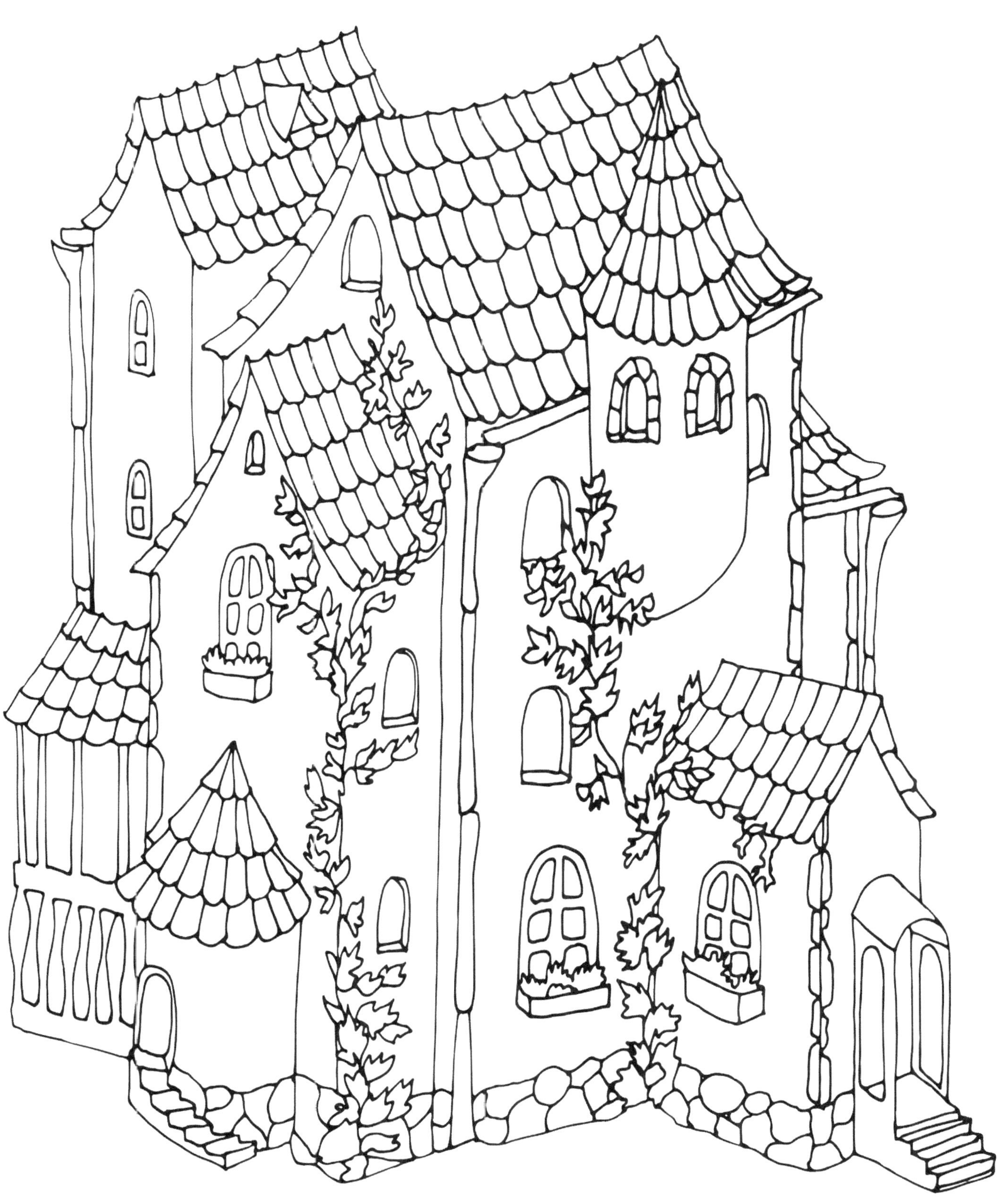

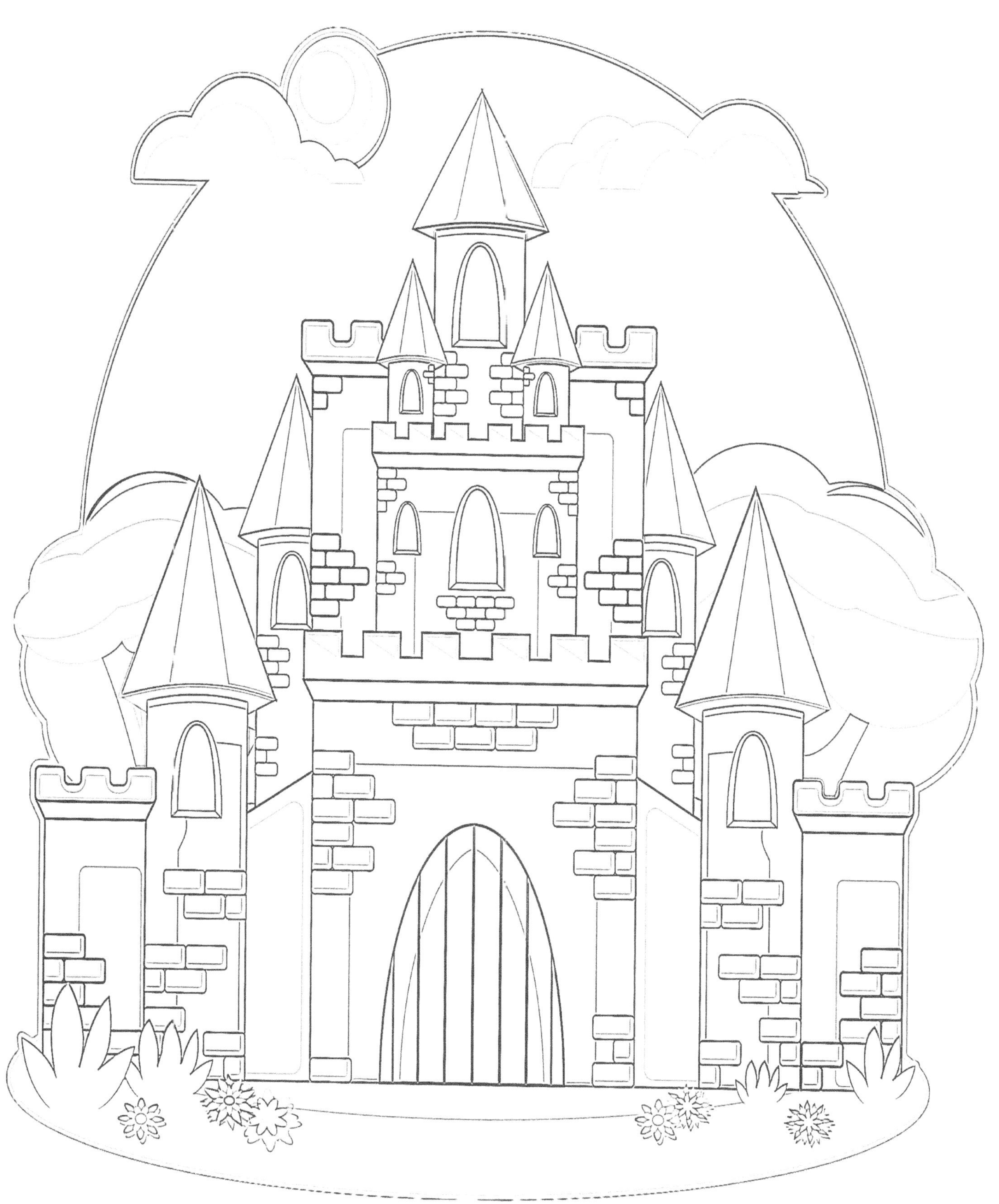

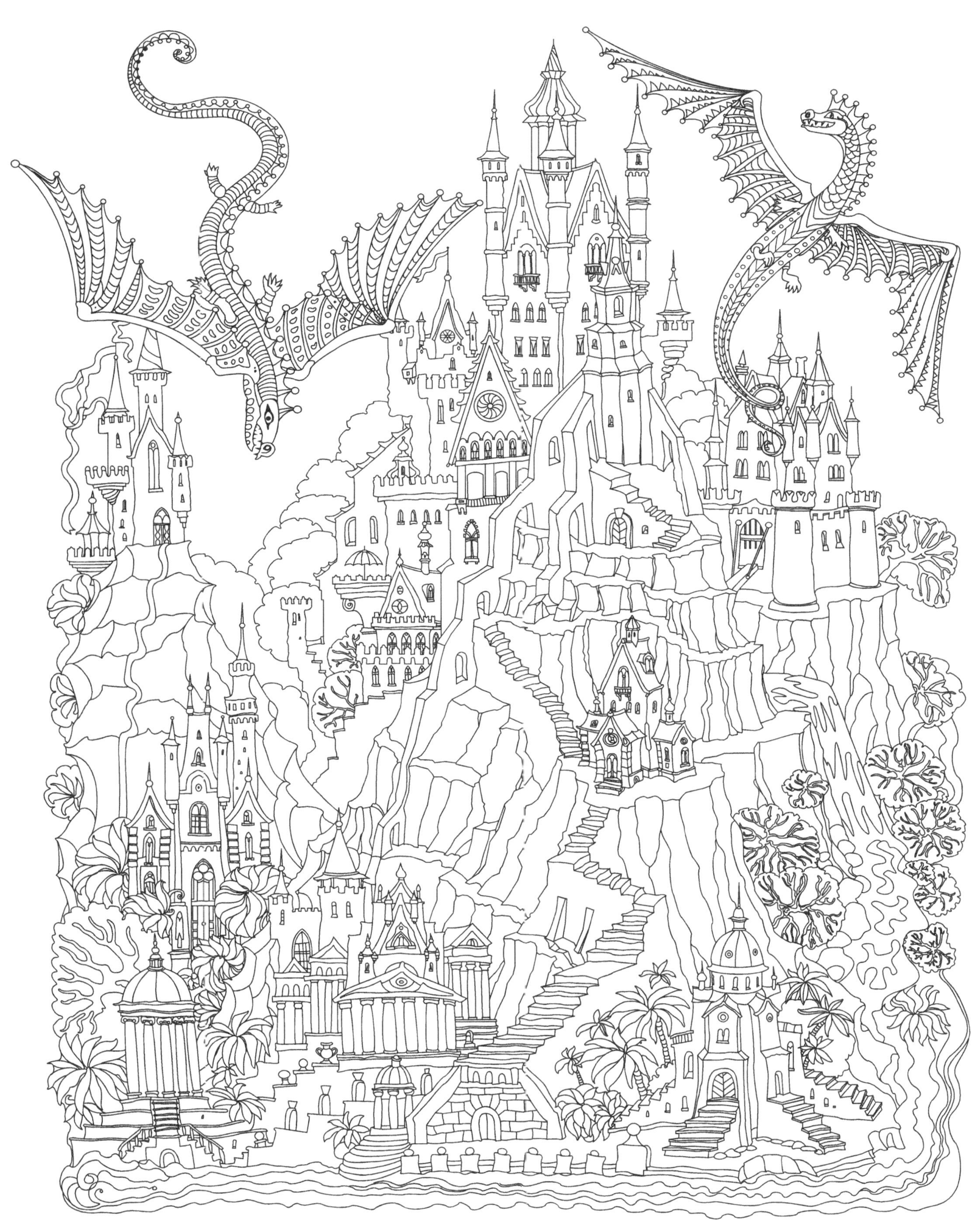

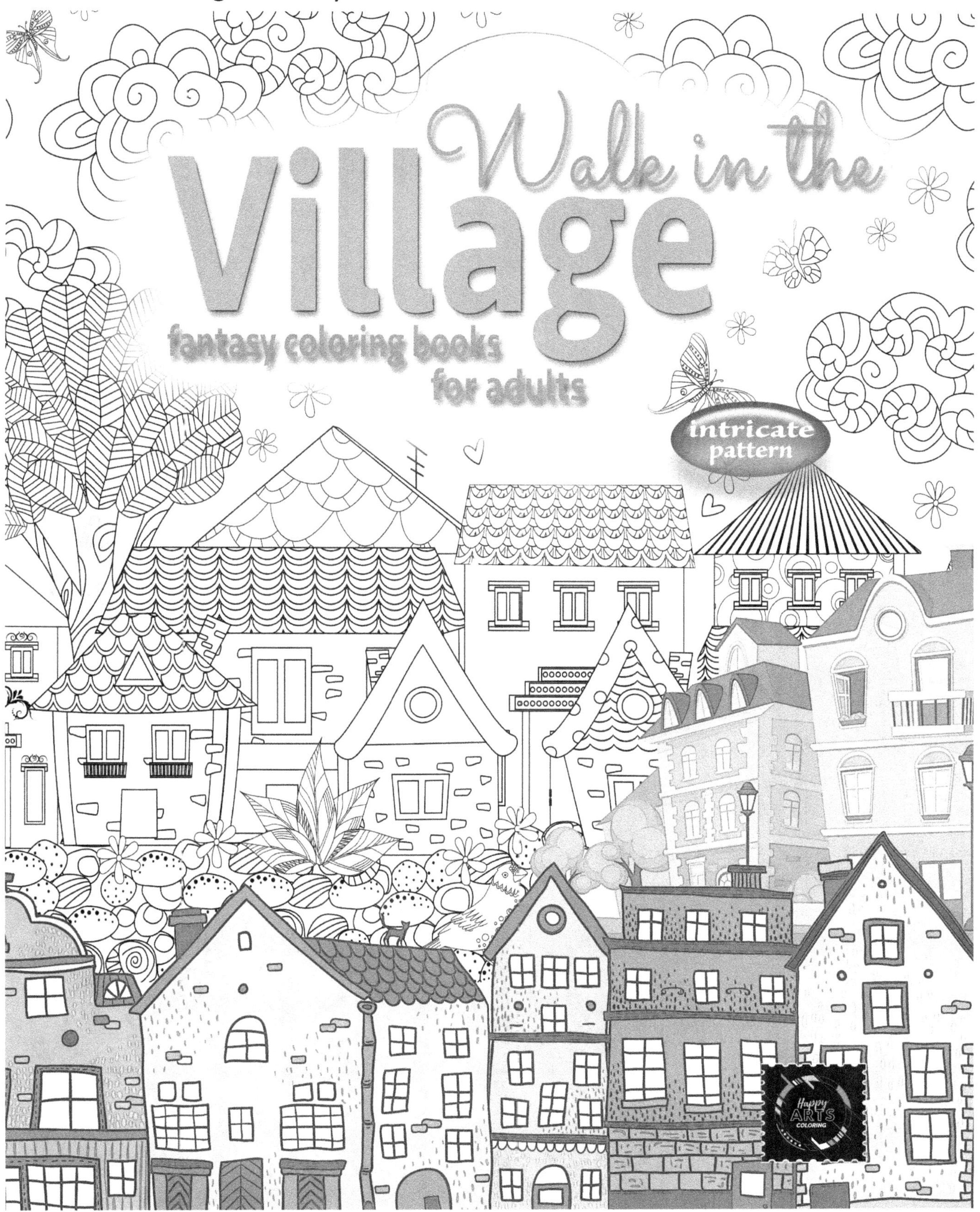
Walk in the
Village
fantasy coloring books
for adults
intricate pattern
Happy ARTS COLORING

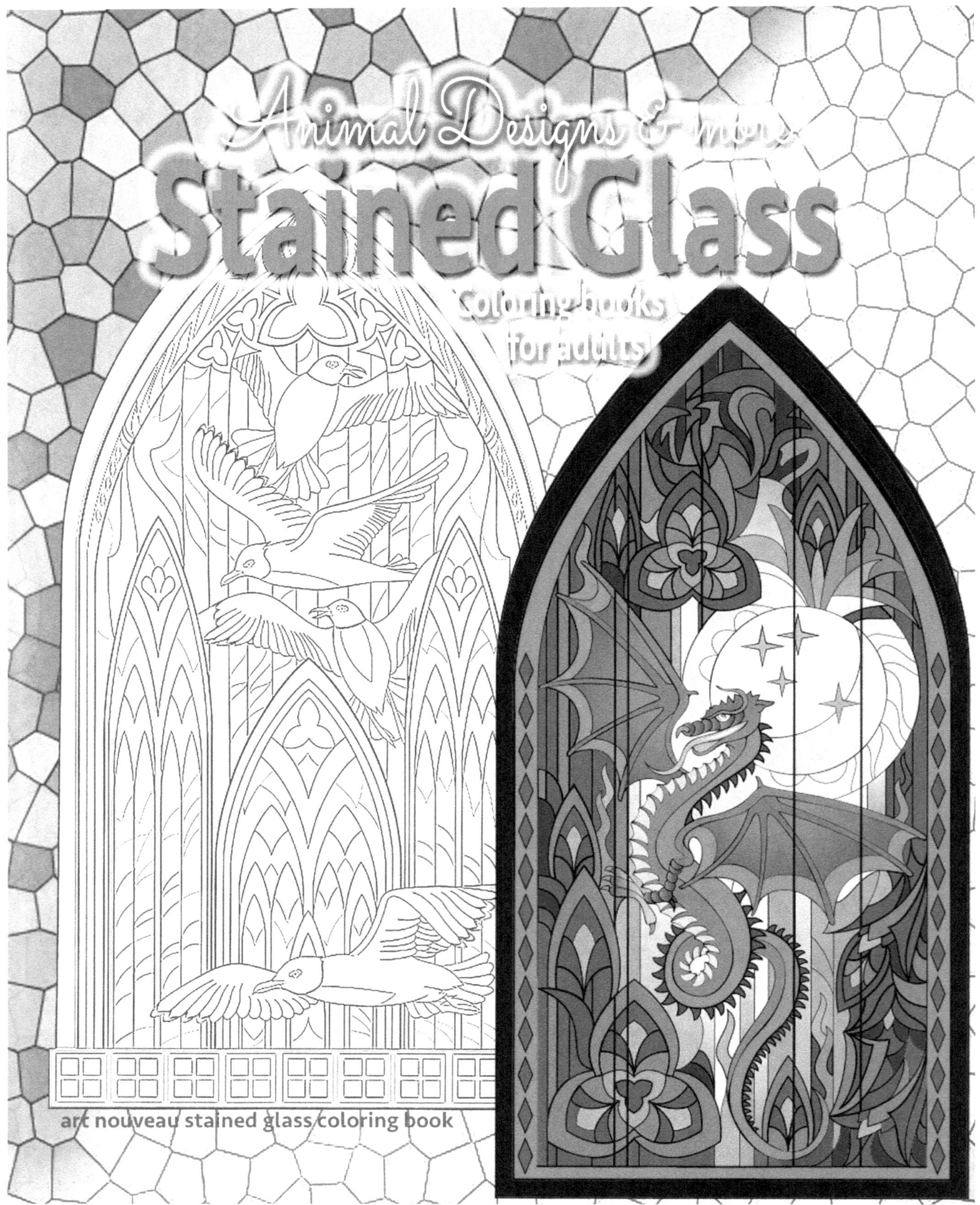
Animal Designs & more
Stained Glass
Coloring books
for adults
art nouveau stained glass coloring book

More Coloring Books by HAPPY ARTS COLORING. Available on AMAZON.

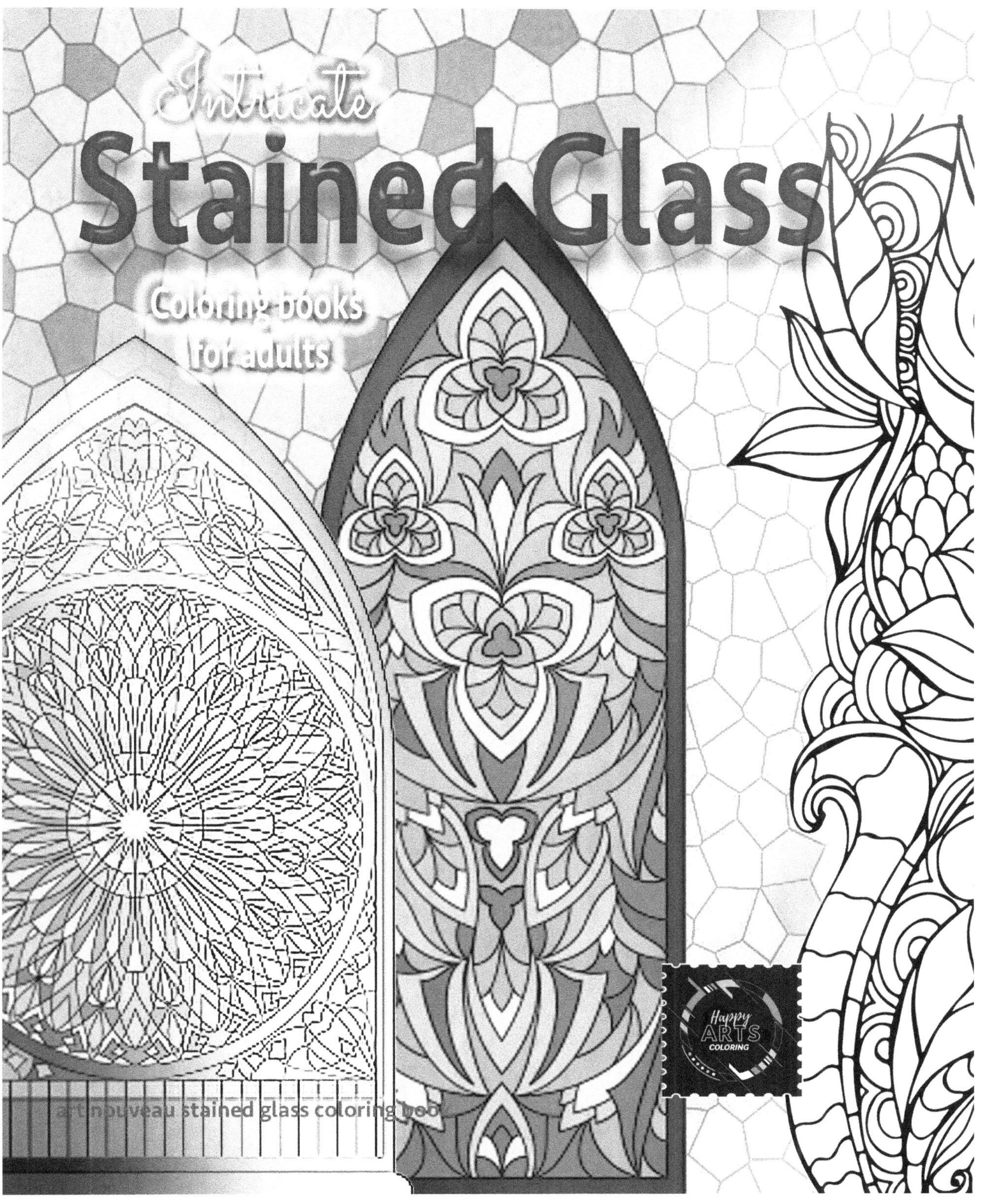

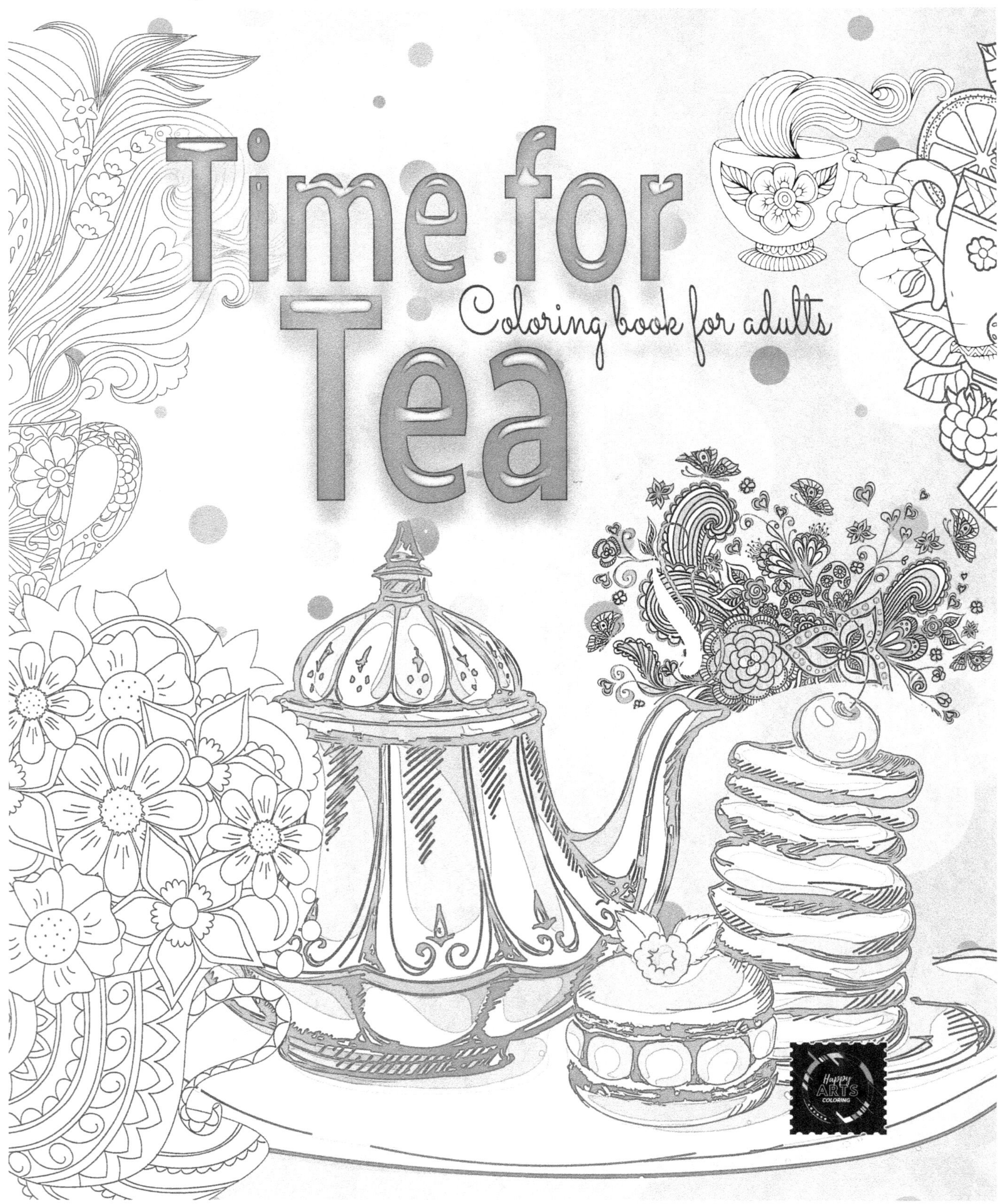
Time for
Tea
Coloring book for adults
Happy
ARTS
COLORING

More Coloring Books by HAPPY ARTS COLORING. Available on AMAZON.

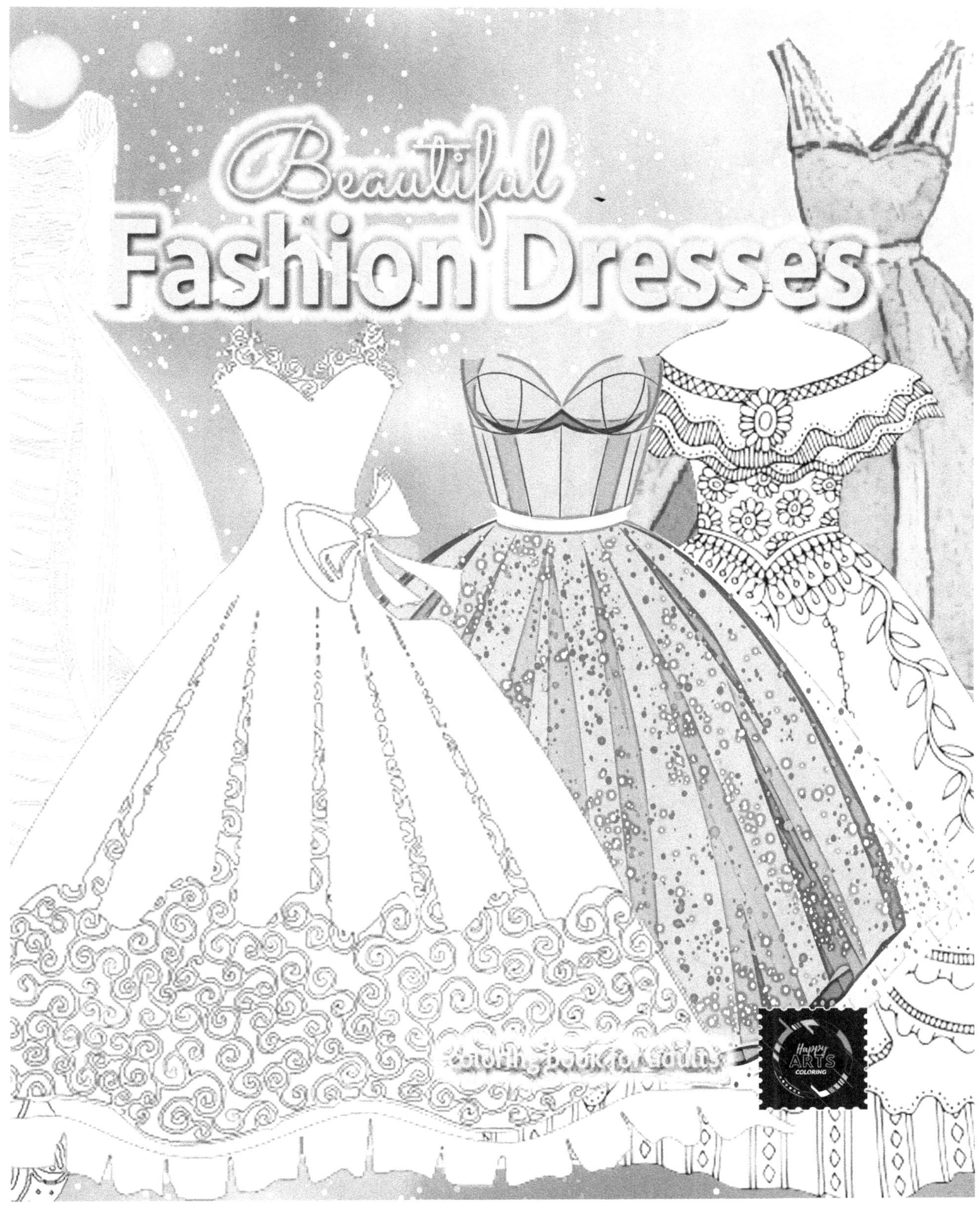

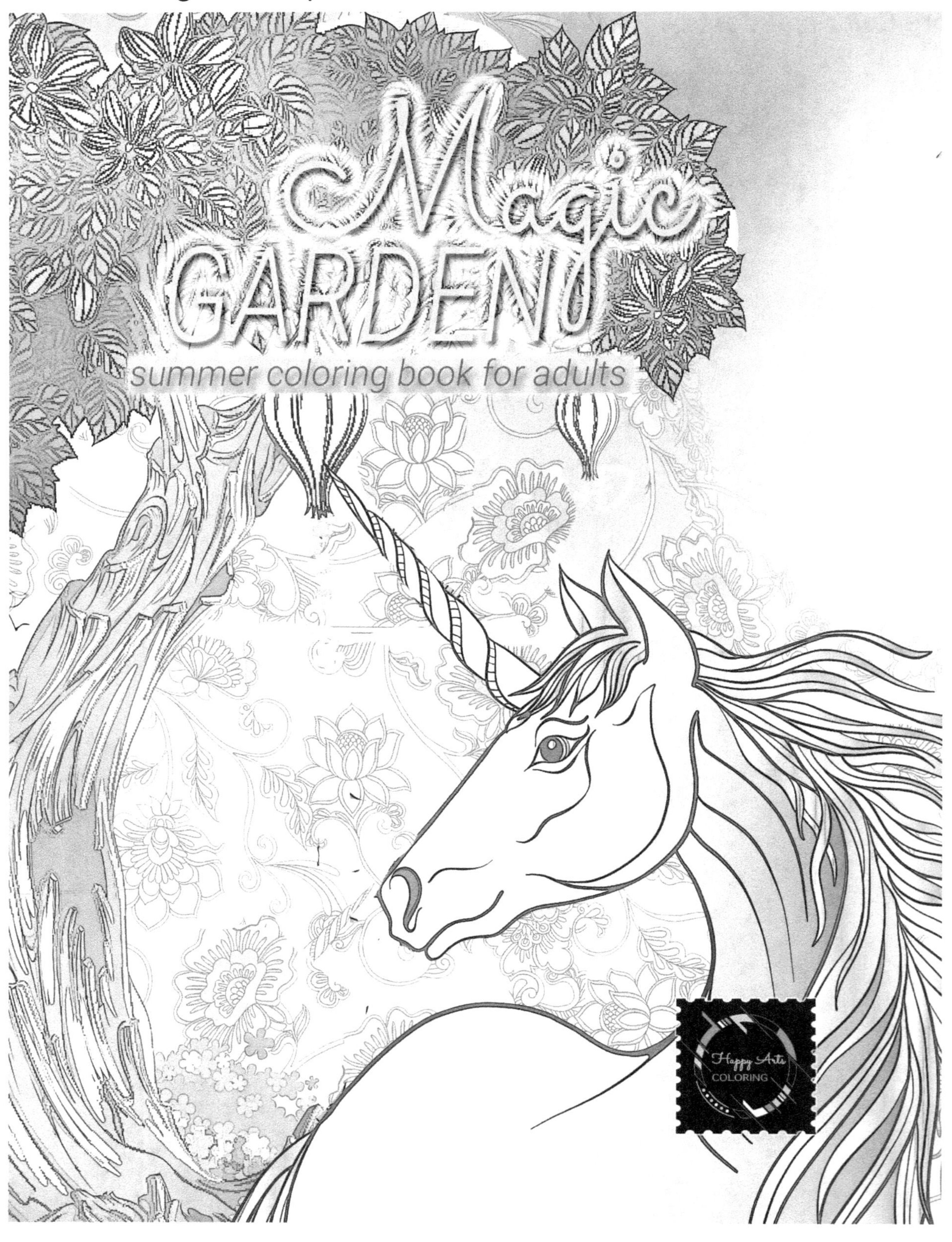
Magic
GARDEN
summer coloring book for adults
Happy Arts
COLORING